WILLIA

The Prophets
Speak Today

*Selections on Contemporary Themes
for Prayer and Reflection*

Nihil Obstat:
>Rev. Hilarion Kistner, O.F.M.
>Rev. John J. Jennings

Imprimi Potest:
>Rev. Andrew Fox, O.F.M.
>Provincial

Imprimatur:
>+Daniel E. Pilarczyk, V.G.
>Archdiocese of Cincinnati
>October 31, 1980

The *Nihil Obstat* and *Imprimatur* are a declaration that a book or pamphlet is considered to be free from doctrinal or moral error. It is not implied that those who have granted the *Nihil Obstat* and *Imprimatur* agree with the contents, opinions or statements expressed.

Cover, book design and illustrations by Julie Van Leeuwen.

SBN 0-912228-82-2

© 1981 St. Anthony Messenger Press
All rights reserved.
Printed in the U.S.A.

Yes, as the rain and the snow
come down from the heavens
and do not return
without watering the earth,
making it yield
and giving growth
to provide seed for the sower
and bread for the eating,
so the word that goes from my mouth
does not return to me empty,
without carrying out my will
and succeeding in what it was sent to do.

Isaiah 55:10-11

Acknowledgments

The biblical texts are taken from *The Jerusalem Bible* except where otherwise indicated. I am grateful to Doubleday and Company, publishers of *The Jerusalem Bible,* and to the Confraternity of Christian Doctrine, copyright owner of *The New American Bible* (NAB), for permission to reproduce the texts that appear in this book.

I wish to thank Father Jeremy Harrington, O.F.M., publisher of St. Anthony Messenger Press, as well as Ms. Karen Hurley and Ms. Carol Luebering, editors, for their continued encouragement and many valuable suggestions. Special thanks are due to my wife Challon for her editorial work and her incisive critique of the book in its various stages.

I am also grateful to my colleagues, Dr. Conrad L'Heureux, professor of Old Testament Studies at the University of Dayton, and Father Greg Tajchman, O.F.M., professor of Old Testament Studies at St. Leonard College, Centerville, Ohio, for reading the entire manuscript and providing helpful comments.

Finally, a sincere word of appreciation goes to my former student, Bill Johnson, for his secretarial assistance, and to Suzanne Ksycewski for typing the manuscript.

*In loving dedication
to my daughters,
Carolyn, Laura and Kathryn*

Foreword

The Hebrew prophets were impassioned persons who intimately experienced God and who were consumed with a deep love and concern for his people. As a consequence, they anguished over the plight of the Israelites in times of crisis. They were consumed by the desire that the people achieve all the blessings that God wished to shower on them. This zeal led the prophets to cry out the message of God to the people of their day.

Unfortunately, the Hebrew prophets have remained strangers to most of the Christian community, even though contemporary biblical studies have deepened understanding of their richness and significance. This scholarship has made seminary and university courses on the prophets more relevant. It has enriched the spirituality of many professionals in the religious realm. But the prophets' message has yet to reach the average layperson.

Of course the prophets' words had a particular significance for the Israelites of the ancient world. Yet modern readers discover that the prophets' message has a universal dimension valid for all time.

The purpose of this book is to bring to a wider

audience significant prophetic texts that proclaim this timeless message in a format that does not demand familiarity with the historical and cultural background of the prophets' world.

Selected texts have therefore been arranged according to seven themes significant for living one's faith today. Each section is preceded by a short introduction and concludes with a reflection on the implications of the prophetic passages for contemporary spirituality. These reflections have been kept brief so that, as much as possible, the prophetic passages might speak for themselves.

So designed, the book is suitable for thematic reading according to the particular mood or felt need of the moment. It can also be used for private or for group prayer.

Private prayer might take one of three forms: 1) slowly and rhythmically reading a selected passage in a prayerful mood; 2) reading a passage, analyzing what it means in terms of one's own perception of God or in terms of its implications for one's own life, and then ending with a brief prayer; 3) reading the passage and then spontaneously talking to God about the selection.

Any of these forms could also be used for informal group prayer, allowing an opportunity for the participants to share with the group their feelings, thoughts or spontaneous prayer based on the selected passage. A more formal Scripture service could also be built around the reading of two or three related passages with time for quiet reflection, a homily and some hymns and recited prayers.

The selections in the book could also provide

ample material for days of recollection or a retreat. Finally, the suggestions at the end of each section can aid personal reflection or group discussion in the classroom, adult enrichment and home study situations.

Contents

Introduction

This introduction provides some minimal background on the prophets to aid in achieving the goals of this book. A glossary containing some of the less familiar terms that appear in the prophetic passages can be found at the end of the book.

The Meaning of Prophet

The word *prophet* is a translation of the Hebrew word *nabi,* which means either "he who is called" or "he who proclaims." These two meanings together describe the essence of prophecy in Israel. The Israelite prophet was one called by God to proclaim and interpret the Word of God.

The Prophetical Books

In most editions of the Bible, 18 books are listed as prophetical works. Six are known as the *major prophets* because of their length: Isaiah, Jeremiah, Lamentations, Baruch, Ezekiel and Daniel. The *minor prophets,* the 12 short books, are: Hosea, Joel, Amos, Obadiah, Jonah, Micah, Nahum, Habbakuk, Zephaniah, Haggai, Zechariah and Malachi.

A Brief Summary of Israelite History*

c. 1800-1500 B.C.: The period of the Patriarchs, including Abraham, Isaac and Jacob.

c. 1300-1200 B.C.: The deliverance of the Israelites under Moses from enslavement in Egypt and the conquest of the promised land under Moses' successor, Joshua.

c. 1200-1050 B.C.: The period of the Judges. During this period Yahweh was considered the ruler of the Israelites. From time to time charismatic leaders known as judges emerged to guide the people through periods of crisis.

c. 1020-1000 B.C.: The beginning of the monarchy with King Saul.

1000-962 B.C.: The rule of King David.

961-922 B.C.: The reign of Solomon, son of David.

922 B.C.: The division of the kingdom into the Northern Kingdom

---

*Most of the dates provided here and in the following summary on the prophets are based on those given in *The Jerome Biblical Commentary*.

(Israel) and the Southern
Kingdom (Judah).

721 B.C.: The Assyrian conquest of
Samaria, capital of the
Northern Kingdom, marking
an end to the Kingdom of
Israel.

640-609 B.C.: The reign of Josiah, King of
Judah.

621 B.C.: Josiah's religious reform to
bring the people back to better observance of the Mosaic
Law.

597 B.C.: The Babylonian seige of Jerusalem, capital of Judah.

587 B.C.: The downfall of the Kingdom
of Judah, with the destruction by the Babylonians of
the city of Jerusalem and the
Temple. Many of the inhabitants were deported to Babylon (the Exile).

539 B.C.: The armies of Cyrus, King of
the Medes and Persians, enter
Babylon.

538 B.C.: The edict of Cyrus, allowing
the return of the exiles to
Judah.

538-333 B.C.: The period following the
Exile. The city of Jerusalem

and the Temple were re-
stored. Palestine was under
Persian dominion.

333-63 B.C.:   The period in which the
Greeks held dominion in the
Near East.

63 B.C. - 135 A.D.:   Palestine under Roman
control.

Situating the Prophets

Given this time line, the prophets excerpted in
this book can be situated in the context of Israelite history:

Amos was a shepherd of Tekoa on the edge of the
desert of Judah. He exercised his brief prophetic
ministry around 750 B.C. in Bethel and Samaria in
the Northern Kingdom. Amos is especially known
for his concern for social justice.

Hosea was from the Northern Kingdom. His prophetic activity took place from about 750 until
after 732 B.C. He is particularly noteworthy for
his use of the metaphor of human marriage to
describe the relationship between Yahweh and
Israel.

Isaiah, the author of much of the first 39 chapters of the Book of Isaiah, was a citizen of Judah.
He received his prophetic call in 742 B.C. and
prophesied until about 701 B.C. He probably exercised all of his prophetic activity in Jerusalem.
His task was to guide Judah through the critical
period of Assyrian ascendancy in the Near East.

Micah, the last of the four great prophets of the eighth century B.C., was from Judah, and exercised his prophetic ministry during the approximate period 740 - 700 B.C. It is likely that he belonged to the peasant class. Like Amos, he championed the cause of the oppressed and needy.

Zephaniah prophesied between 640 and 630 B.C., prior to the reform of Josiah and the prophetic ministry of Jeremiah.

Jeremiah witnessed the fall of the Assyrian empire and the rising of the Babylonian empire. In 626 B.C. at the age of 20, he was called to be a prophet in the midst of these political upheavals. His prophetic activity extended from before the reform of Josiah until after the destruction of Judah in 587 B.C. and the beginning of the Babylonian Exile.

Ezekiel prophesied between 593 and 571 B.C. Much of his prophetic ministry was exercised among the exiles in Babylon. He was both priest and prophet, poet and theologian. His prophecies are especially rich with highly symbolic imagery.

Second Isaiah is an anonymous prophet responsible for chapters 40-55 of the Book of Isaiah. He addressed his prophetic proclamations to the exiles in Babylon during the latter part of the exilic period (550-540 B.C.). Because of Second Isaiah's message of hope to the exiles, these chapters are referred to as the Book of Consolation. This prophet probably belonged to an Isaian school of religious thought, for his work echoes the earlier Isaiah's thinking.

Third Isaiah is the name given to the prophet or group of prophets who authored chapters 56-66 of the Book of Isaiah. These chapters are dated after 515 B.C. Third Isaiah integrated the message of Second Isaiah with the new situation of post-exilic Israel.

Zechariah, the author of chapters 1-8 of the Book of Zechariah, was probably born in a priestly family. He exercised his prophetic ministry at least from October or November, 520, until November, 518 B.C., during the early years after the return from the Babylonian Exile.

Second Zechariah is responsible for chapters 9-14 of the Book of Zechariah. These chapters were written later in the post-exilic period.

Joel prophesied between 400 and 350 B.C. He may have been attached to the Temple as a spokesman for Yahweh and the community. Especially noteworthy is his prophesy of the outpouring of the Spirit on all humankind (3:1).

For Further Reading
Many references are available for those who wish more detailed background.

For a short and readable introduction to the prophets, any one of the following would be helpful: Wilfrid Harrington's *Key to the Bible,* vol. 2, pp. 43-83 (Alba Books); *Israel's Prophets: Envoys of the King,* by Walter Wifall (Franciscan Herald Press); *The Dimension Bible Guides,* Vols. 8 and

9, by E.H. Robertson, and vol. 10, by H.G.G. Herklots (Dimension Books).

A more exhaustive and scholarly treatment of the prophets can be found in *The Prophets,* vols. 1 and 2, by Abraham Heschel (Harper and Row); *The Conscience of Israel,* by Bruce Vawter; (Sheed and Ward); and the articles on the prophets in *The Jerome Biblical Commentary.*

I. God's Call

The selections in this section are taken from passages in which a prophet describes the commission (the "call") he receives from God to proclaim the divine word to the people of his time. The general introduction to the book situates historically the call of each of the five prophets represented here.

Isaiah 6:1-8

In the year King Uzziah died, I saw the Lord seated on a high and lofty throne, with the train of his garment filling the temple. Seraphim were stationed above; each of them had six wings: with two they veiled their faces, with two they veiled their feet, and with two they hovered aloft.

"Holy, holy, holy is the LORD of hosts!" they cried one to the other. "All the earth is filled with his glory!" At the sound of that cry, the frame of the door shook and the house was filled with smoke.

Then I said, "Woe is me, I am doomed! For I am a man of unclean lips, living among a people of unclean lips; yet my eyes have seen the King, the LORD of hosts!" Then one of the seraphim flew to me, holding an ember which he had taken with tongs from the altar.

He touched my mouth with it. "See," he said, "now that this has touched your lips, your wickedness is removed, your sin purged."

Then I heard the voice of the Lord saying, "Whom shall I send? Who will go for us?" "Here I am," I said; "send me!"

(NAB)

Jeremiah 1:4-10

The word of Yahweh was addressed to me, saying,

"Before I formed you in the womb I knew
*   you;*
before you came to birth I consecrated you;
I have appointed you as a prophet to the
*   nations."*

I said, "Ah, Lord Yahweh; look, I do not
know how to speak: I am a child!"

But Yahweh replied,
"Do not say, 'I am a child.'
Go now to those to whom I send you
and say whatever I command you.
Do not be afraid of them,
for I am with you to protect you—
it is Yahweh who speaks!"

Then Yahweh put out his hand and touched
my mouth and said to me:

"There! I am putting my words into your
*   mouth.*
Look, today I am setting you
over nations and over kingdoms,
to tear up and to knock down,
to destroy and to overthrow,
to build and to plant."

Ezekiel 2:8—3:3

"You, son of man, listen to the words I say; do not be a rebel like that rebellious set. Open your mouth and eat what I am about to give you." I looked. A hand was there, stretching out to me and holding a scroll. He unrolled it in front of me; it was written on back and front; on it was written "lamentations, wailings, moanings." He said, "Son of man, eat what is given to you; eat this scroll, then go and speak to the House of Israel." I opened my mouth; he gave me the scroll to eat and said, "Son of man, feed and be satisfied by the scroll I am giving you." I ate it, and it tasted sweet as honey.

Isaiah 40:1-11

"Console my people, console them,"
says your God.
"Speak to the heart of Jerusalem
and call to her
that her time of service is ended,
that her sin is atoned for,
that she has received from the hand of Yahweh
double punishment for all her crimes."

A voice cries, "Prepare in the wilderness
a way for Yahweh.
Make a straight highway for our God
across the desert.

Let every valley be filled in,
every mountain and hill be laid low,
let every cliff become a plain,
and the ridges a valley;
then the glory of Yahweh shall be revealed
and all mankind shall see it;
for the mouth of Yahweh has spoken."
A voice commands: "Cry!"
and I answered, "What shall I cry?"
—"All flesh is grass
and its beauty like the wild flower's.
The grass withers, the flower fades
when the breath of Yahweh blows on them.
(The grass is without doubt the people.)
The grass withers, the flower fades,
but the word of our God remains for ever."

Go up on a high mountain,
joyful messenger to Zion,
Shout with a loud voice,
joyful messenger to Jerusalem.
Shout without fear,
say to the towns of Judah,
"Here is your God."

Here is the Lord Yahweh coming with power,
his arm subduing all things to him.
The prize of his victory is with him,
his trophies all go before him.
He is like a shepherd feeding his flock,
gathering lambs in his arms,
holding them against his breast
and leading to their rest the mother ewes.

Isaiah 61:1-11

The spirit of the Lord Yahweh has been given to me
me,
for Yahweh has anointed me.
He has sent me to bring good news to the poor,
to bind up hearts that are broken;

to proclaim liberty to captives,
freedom to those in prison;
to proclaim a year of favor from Yahweh,
a day of vengeance for our God,

to comfort all those who mourn and to give them
for ashes a garland;
for mourning robe the oil of gladness,
for despondency, praise.
They are to be called "terebinths of integrity,"
planted by Yahweh to glorify him.

They will rebuild the ancient ruins,
they will raise what has long lain waste,
they will restore the ruined cities,
all that has lain waste for ages past.

Strangers will be there to feed your flocks,
foreigners as your plowmen and vinedressers;
but you, you will be named "priests of Yahweh,"
they will call you "ministers of our God."
You will feed on the wealth of nations
and array yourselves in their magnificence.

For their shame was twofold,
disgrace and spitting their lot.
Twofold therefore shall they possess in their land,
everlasting joy is theirs.

For I, Yahweh, love justice,
I hate robbery and all that is wrong.
I reward them faithfully
and make an everlasting covenant with them.

Their race will be famous throughout the nations,
their descendants throughout the peoples.
All who see them will admit
that they are a race whom Yahweh has blessed.

"I exult for joy in Yahweh,
my soul rejoices in my God,
for he has clothed me in the garments of salvation,
he has wrapped me in the cloak of integrity,
like a bridegroom wearing his wreath,
like a bride adorned in her jewels.

"For as the earth makes fresh things grow,
as a garden makes seeds spring up,
so will the Lord Yahweh make both integrity
    and praise
spring up in the sight of the nations."

Implications for Today

From these testimonies of the experience of God's call, there emerges a rather comprehensive picture of the prophetic vocation. The call is always at the initiative of God, who communicates his word and his spirit to the prophet. The commission is given to announce God's word in season and out of season. Sometimes the word to be proclaimed is one of judgment, sometimes one of consolation, but always the word challenges us to strive for a better life.

After experiencing God's presence and listening to the divine communication, the first reaction on the part of the prophet is often one of unworthiness or inadequacy. This is followed by an experience of the power of God that brings about an inner transformation. Strengthened by God's grace, the prophet responds in an open-ended commitment, "Here I am, send me!"

In the *Dogmatic Constitution on the Church* the Second Vatican Council speaks of the call of the people of God to share in the prophetic mission of Christ (see # 12). It is valuable to reflect on one's own vocation in accord with the elements revealed in the prophets' descriptions of their own calling.

For Reflection and Discussion

Compare Isaiah 61:1-2 with the following
New Testament texts: Matthew 3:16-17; 11:
2-6; Luke 4:16-22; 7:18-23; John 1:29-33.

What elements of divine vocation, as manifested in the prophetic selections in this section,
can you identify in your own call by God?

What is the prophetic dimension in the baptismal call of every Christian?

What are some of the ordinary ways in which a
person can live out this prophetic vocation
within the context of one's basic lifestyle
(married, celibate, single) and one's daily occu-
pation (e.g., teaching, business, factory work,
service profession)?

Describe some extraordinary ways in which
one might be called to be prophetic in today's
world.

II. God's Faithful Love

All the selections in this section are from the period of the Babylonian Exile or shortly thereafter. It is significant that in one of the darkest hours of Israelite history the prophets spoke so poignantly to the people about God's unshakable love and personal concern.

Isaiah 43:1-3

Do not be afraid, for I have redeemed you;
I have called you by your name, you are mine.
Should you pass through the sea, I will be with
*   you;*
or through rivers, they will not swallow you up.
Should you walk through fire, you will not be
*   scorched*
and the flames will not burn you.
For I am Yahweh, your God,
the Holy One of Israel, your savior.

Isaiah 43:11-13

I, I am Yahweh,
there is no other savior but me.
It is I who have spoken, have saved, have made
*   the proclamation,*
not any strangers among you.
You are my witnesses—it is Yahweh who speaks—
and I, I am your God, I am he from eternity.
No one can deliver from my hand,
I act and no one can reverse it.

Ezekiel 34:11-16

For the Lord Yahweh says this: I am going to look after my flock myself and keep all of it in view. As a shepherd keeps all his flock in view when he stands up in the middle of his scattered sheep, so shall I keep my sheep in view. I shall rescue them from wherever they have been scattered during the mist and darkness. I shall bring them out of the countries where they are; I shall gather them together from foreign countries and bring them back to their own land. I shall pasture them on the mountains of Israel, in the ravines and in every inhabited place in the land. I shall feed them in good pasturage; the high mountains of Israel will be their grazing ground. There they will rest in good grazing ground; they will browse in rich pastures on the mountains of Israel. I myself will pasture my sheep, I myself will show them where to rest—it is the Lord Yahweh who speaks. I shall look for the lost one, bring back the stray, bandage the wounded and make the weak strong. I shall watch over the fat and healthy. I shall be a true shepherd to them.

Isaiah 55:1-3

Oh, come to the water all you who are thirsty;
though you have no money, come!
Buy corn without money, and eat,
and, at no cost, wine and milk.
Why spend money on what is not bread,
your wages on what fails to satisfy?
Listen, listen to me, and you will have good
*   things to eat*
and rich food to enjoy.
Pay attention, come to me;
listen, and your soul will live.

Isaiah 54:5

For now your creator will be your husband,
his name, Yahweh Sabaoth;
your redeemer will be the Holy One of Israel,
he is called the God of the whole earth.

Isaiah 41:10

Do not be afraid, for I am with you;
stop being anxious and watchful, for I am your
*   God.*
I give you strength, I bring you help,
I uphold you with my victorious right hand.

Hosea 2:18-22

When that day comes—it is Yahweh who speaks—
she [Israel] will call me "My husband,"
no longer will she call me "My Baal."
I will take the names of the Baals off her lips,
their names shall never be uttered again.

When that day comes I will make a treaty on
*   her behalf with the wild animals,*
with the birds of heaven and the creeping things
*   of the earth;*
I will break bow, sword and battle in the country,
and make her sleep secure.
I will betroth you to myself for ever,
betroth you with integrity and justice,
with tenderness and love;
I will betroth you to myself with faithfulness,
and you will come to know Yahweh.

Isaiah 66:9

Am I to open the womb and not bring to birth?
  says Yahweh.
Or I, who bring to birth, am I to close it?
  says your God.

Isaiah 51:14-16

*The captive is soon to be set free; he will not
die in a deep dungeon nor will his bread run out.
I am Yahweh your God who stirs the sea, making
its waves roar, my name is Yahweh Sabaoth. I put
my words into your mouth, I hid you in the shadow of my hand, when I spread out the heavens
and laid the earth's foundations and said to Zion,
"You are my people."*

Hosea 11:1-4

When Israel was a child I loved him,
  out of Egypt I called my son.
The more I called them,
  the farther they went from me,
Sacrificing to the Baals
  and burning incense to idols.
Yet it was I who taught Ephraim to walk,
  who took them in my arms;
I drew them with human cords,
  with bands of love;
I fostered them like one
  who raises an infant to his cheeks;
Yet, though I stooped to feed my child,
  they did not know that I was their healer.

(NAB)

Isaiah 49:15-16

Does a woman forget her baby at the breast,
or fail to cherish the son of her womb?
Yet even if these forget,
I will never forget you.

See, I have branded you on the palms of my
*   hands,*
your ramparts are always under my eye.

Isaiah 46:4

"In your old age I shall be still the same,
when your hair is gray I shall still support you.
I have already done so, I have carried you,
I shall still support and deliver you."

Isaiah 54:10

. . . For the mountains may depart,
the hills be shaken,
but my love for you will never leave you
and my covenant of peace with you will never
    be shaken,
says Yahweh who takes pity on you.

Implications for Today

The prophets of the exilic period preached to a people who had experienced profound human tragedy. The capital city of Jerusalem and the Temple had been destroyed and the people were driven into exile. In such times hard questions, come to mind: Where is God? Why has God abandoned us?

The prophetic proclamations confront these questions directly: "I hid you in the shadow of my hand." "I carried you, I shall still support and deliver you." Because of a profound awareness of God's love, the prophets were able to live through one of the most tragic periods of Israelite history without ever losing faith in God's covenant relationship with his people.

The experience of God's intimate love for each person is the most important basis upon which a total faith life is built. Too frequently this divine love is reduced to an abstract quality or a general kind of love that God has for all creation. The most difficult and threatening challenge is to believe in one's own lovableness before God, to take seriously how much one's own person means to God.

Awareness of God's personal love should become the central focus of prayer, preaching and religious formation. Only in the context of a deep conviction of God's intimate and unbreakable love can all other aspects of a religious belief and practice be perceived in a healthful perspective and all the diverse realities of life—even the most bitter—be experienced in a redemptive way.

For Reflection and Discussion

Compare Ezekiel 34:11-16 with John 10:1-18.

In the light of the passages in this section, comment on the often-heard statement, "The God of the Old Testament is a God of fear and wrath; the God of the New Testament is a God of love."

Select from these passages those verses that speak most poignantly to you of the intimacy of God's personal love.

Compare your own concept of God's love for you with the prophetic view of divine love presented in this section.

What elements in your spiritual life reflect belief in God's love for you as described by the prophets? What elements manifest a view of God as an unloving dispenser of judgment?

How can faith in God's personal love influence the way in which one experiences sorrow and tragedy? Illustrate by concrete examples.

III. God's Justice

A perennial problem in the history of religion has been the tendency to identify mere external religious observance with holiness. The Israelites were not immune from this temptation. Many of them had reduced the challenge of living in a covenant relationship with God to fulfilling the outward details of ritual practice. In the meantime they neglected turning their hearts to God and to their neighbor. The prophets had to remind them that response to God's covenant really implies a total conversion.

Hosea 10:12

Sow integrity for yourselves,
reap a harvest of kindness,
break up your fallow ground:
it is time to go seeking Yahweh
until he comes to rain salvation on you.

Amos 5:21-24

I hate, I spurn your feasts,
  I take no pleasure in your solemnities;
Your cereal offerings I will not accept,
  nor consider your stall-fed peace offerings.
Away with your noisy songs!
  I will not listen to the melodies of your harps.
But if you would offer me holocausts,
  then let justice surge like water,
  and goodness like an unfailing stream.

(NAB)

Zechariah 7:9-10

Render true judgment, and show kindness and compassion toward each other. Do not oppress the widow or the orphan, the alien or the poor; do not plot evil against one another in your hearts.

(NAB)

Isaiah 1:11-17

"What are your endless sacrifices to me?
says Yahweh.
I am sick of holocausts of rams
and the fat of calves.
The blood of bulls and of goats revolts me.
When you come to present yourselves before me,
who asked you to trample over my courts?
Bring me your worthless offerings no more,
the smoke of them fills me with disgust.
New Moons, sabbaths, assemblies—
I cannot endure festival and solemnity.
Your New Moons and your pilgrimages
I hate with all my soul.
They lie heavy on me,
I am tired of bearing them.
When you stretch out your hands
I turn my eyes away.
You may multiply your prayers,
I shall not listen.
Your hands are covered with blood,
wash, make yourselves clean.

"Take your wrongdoing out of my sight.
Cease to do evil.
Learn to do good,
search for justice,
help the oppressed,
be just to the orphan,
plead for the widow."

Isaiah 26:7-9

The path of the upright man is straight,
you smooth the way of the upright.
Following the path of your judgments,
we hoped in you, Yahweh,
your name, your memory are all my soul desires.

At night my soul longs for you
and my spirit in me seeks for you;
when your judgments appear on earth
the inhabitants of the world learn the meaning
*   of integrity.*

Isaiah 5:20-24

Woe to those who call evil good, and good evil,
who substitute darkness for light
and light for darkness,
who substitute bitter for sweet
and sweet for bitter.

Woe to those who think themselves wise
and believe themselves cunning.
Woe to the heroes of drinking bouts,
to the champions at preparing strong drinks.
Woe to those who for a bribe acquit the guilty
and cheat the good man of his due.
For this, as stubble is prey for the flames
and as straw vanishes in the fire,
so their root will rot,
their blossom be carried off like dust,
for rejecting the Law of Yahweh Sabaoth,
and despising the word of the Holy One of Israel.

Amos 5:14-15

Seek good and not evil
so that you may live,
and that Yahweh, God of Sabaoth, may really
*   be with you*
as you claim he is.
Hate evil, love good,
maintain justice at the city gate,
and it may be that Yahweh, God of Sabaoth,
*   will take pity*
on the remnant of Joseph.

Jeremiah 7:1-11

The following message came to Jeremiah from the LORD: Stand at the gate of the house of the LORD, and there proclaim this message: Hear the word of the LORD, all you of Judah who enter these gates to worship the LORD! Thus says the LORD of hosts, the God of Israel: Reform your ways and your deeds, so that I may remain with you in this place. Put not your trust in the deceitful words: "This is the temple of the LORD! The temple of the LORD! The temple of the LORD!" Only if you thoroughly reform your ways and your deeds; if each of you deals justly with his neighbor; if you no longer oppress the resident alien, the orphan, and the widow; if you no longer shed innocent blood in this place, or follow strange gods to your own harm, will I remain with you in this place, in the land which I gave your fathers long ago and forever.

But here you are, putting your trust in deceitful words to your own loss! Are you to steal and murder, commit adultery and perjury, burn incense to Baal, go after strange gods that you know not, and yet come to stand before me in this house which bears my name, and say: "We are safe; we can commit all these abominations again"? Has this house which bears my name become in your eyes a den of thieves? I too see what is being done, says the LORD.

(NAB)

Amos 5:7, 10-13

Trouble for those who turn justice into worm-
wood,
throwing integrity to the ground;
who hate the man dispensing justice at the city
gate
and detest those who speak with honesty.
Well then, since you have trampled on the poor
man,
extorting levies on his wheat—
those houses you have built of dressed stone,
you will never live in them;
and those precious vineyards you have planted,
you will never drink their wine.
For I know that your crimes are many,
and your sins enormous:
persecutors of the virtuous, blackmailers,
turning away the needy at the city gate.
No wonder the prudent man keeps silent,
the times are so evil.

Jeremiah 9:23-24

"Let the sage boast no more of his wisdom,
nor the valiant of his valor,
nor the rich man of his riches!
But if anyone wants to boast, let him boast of
    this:
of understanding and knowing me.
For I am Yahweh, I rule with kindness,
justice and integrity on earth;
yes, these are what please me
—it is Yahweh who speaks."

Isaiah 10:1-4

Woe to those who enact unjust statutes
*   and who write oppressive decrees,*
Depriving the needy of judgment
*   and robbing my people's poor of their rights,*
Making widows their plunder,
*   and orphans their prey!*
What will you do on the day of punishment,
*   when ruin comes from afar?*
To whom will you flee for help?
*   Where will you leave your wealth,*
Lest it sink beneath the captive
*   or fall beneath the slain?*

(NAB)

Isaiah 58:1-12

Shout for all you are worth,
raise your voice like a trumpet.
Proclaim their faults to my people,
their sins to the House of Jacob.

They seek me day after day,
they long to know my ways,
like a nation that wants to act with integrity
and not ignore the law of its God.

They ask me for laws that are just,
they long for God to draw near:
"Why should we fast if you never see it,
why do penance if you never notice?"

Look, you do business on your fast days,
you oppress all your workmen;
look, you quarrel and squabble when you fast
and strike the poor man with your fist.

Fasting like yours today
will never make your voice heard on high.
Is that the sort of fast that pleases me,
a truly penitential day for men?

Hanging your head like a reed,
lying down on sackcloth and ashes?
Is that what you call fasting,
a day acceptable to Yahweh?

Is not this the sort of fast that pleases me
—it is the Lord Yahweh who speaks—
to break unjust fetters
and undo the thongs of the yoke,

to let the oppressed go free,
and break every yoke,
to share your bread with the hungry,
and shelter the homeless poor,

to clothe the man you see to be naked
and not turn from your own kin?
Then will your light shine like the dawn
and your wound be quickly healed over.

Your integrity will go before you
and the glory of Yahweh behind you.
Cry, and Yahweh will answer;
call, and he will say, "I am here."

If you do away with the yoke,
the clenched fist, the wicked word,
if you give your bread to the hungry,
and relief to the oppressed,

your light will rise in the darkness,
and your shadows become like noon.
Yahweh will always guide you,
giving you relief in desert places.

He will give strength to your bones
and you shall be like a watered garden,
like a spring of water
whose waters never run dry.

You will rebuild the ancient ruins,
build up on the old foundations.
You will be called "Breach-mender,"
"Restorer of ruined houses."

Zechariah 8:16-17

These then are the things you should do: Speak the truth to one another; let there be honesty and peace in the judgments at your gates, and let none of you plot evil against another in his heart, nor love a false oath. For all these things I hate, says the LORD.

(NAB)

Isaiah 30:15

For thus says the Lord Yahweh, the Holy One
  of Israel:
Your salvation lay in conversion and tranquility,
your strength, in complete trust;
and you would have none of it.

Isaiah 56:1

Thus says Yahweh: Have a care for justice, act
with integrity, for soon my salvation will come
and my integrity be manifest.

Micah 6:6-8

—"With what gift shall I come into Yahweh's
  presence
and bow down before God on high?
Shall I come with holocausts,
with calves one year old?
Will he be pleased with rams by the thousand,
with libations of oil in torrents?
Must I give my first-born for what I have done
  wrong,
the fruit of my body for my own sin?"
—What is good has been explained to you, man;
this is what Yahweh asks of you:
only this, to act justly,
to love tenderly
and to walk humbly with your God.

Implications for Today

The Christian reader may be surprised to find love of God and love of neighbor firmly linked centuries before Jesus. Jesus radically broadened the common notion of neighbor in ancient times to make it include one's enemies as well as one's friends and kinsfolk (see Matthew 5:17, 43-48; Luke 10:29-37), but his teaching is very deeply rooted in the prophetic tradition.

The prophetic understanding of authentic holiness stresses the necessary connection between inner acceptance of God and external religious expression. The performance of rituals is meaningless—even perverse—if it does not express an inward response to God's love and a personal commitment to fulfilling God's will.

For the prophet God's will was not some kind of nebulous theory that could be known only through conjecture. Rather, it was simple and clear-cut. There is only one way to live out one's love of God and that is in love of one's neighbor. This love is made manifest by practicing justice, by liberating the oppressed and by caring for the poor and the needy. Only then will one's light "shine like the dawn" and one's wound "be quickly healed over."

Contemporary approaches to spirituality must resist the temptation to measure dedication to God's will in terms of pious exercises and external norms of behavior. What is demanded is to be born of the Spirit who, like the wind, "blows wherever it pleases" (John 3:8).

The modern believer cannot pretend that religious obligations and social responsibilities are separable realities. Allowing God to come into one's life must involve a concerned welcome to those whom God has called as his very own, especially the lost, the impoverished, the neglected. The worship service brings one closer to God only if it extends into increased service to those with whom God has forever pitched his tent.

For Reflection and Discussion

Compare the prophetic view of authentic religion in the foregoing passages with the following New Testament texts: Matthew 6: 1-8, 23:1-32, 25:31-46; Mark 7:1-23; James 1: 26-27.

Identify those vices which the prophets perceive as most alien to true religion.

Enumerate the virtues and practices that are considered by the prophets as essential components of genuine holiness.

Describe the moral evils and virtues that have been most emphasized in the religious training and preaching to which you have been exposed. Compare this with your answers to the above two questions.

Can the prophets be used as a support for this opinion: "It is not necessary to go to church, pray, or fast; the only thing important is to live a good life"? Explain.

In light of the passages in this section, comment on the following statement: "The preacher should speak about the things of God, *not* use the pulpit to talk about social issues."

IV. God's Promise of Salvation

A very large proportion of prophetic utterances center on the theme of hope. This observation becomes even more striking when it is recalled that almost all of these expressions of optimism were uttered during two of the most critical periods in the history of the Israelite people. Approximately half of the selections in this section originated in the eighth century, B.C. It was during this century that the Assyrian conquest of Israel and the destruction of the Northern Kingdom occurred. Most of the remaining oracles come from the sixth century, B.C., the period of the Babylonian conquest of Judah and the exile.

In neither period was there much visible cause for trusting in a new beginning. All past expectations seemed forever dashed to the ground. Yet in the midst of the darkness the prophets saw light. Despite all the reasons for despair, the prophets looked beyond the tangible and believed that God would indeed raise up new life from the dry bones.

Micah 7:7

For my part, I look to Yahweh,
my hope is in the God who will save me;
my God will hear me.

Isaiah 49:8-13

Thus says Yahweh:
At the favorable time I will answer you,
on the day of salvation I will help you.
(I have formed you and have appointed you
as covenant of the people.)
I will restore the land
and assign you the estates that lie waste.
I will say to the prisoners, "Come out,"
to those who are in darkness, "Show yourselves."

On every roadway they will graze,
and each bare height shall be their pasture.
They will never hunger or thirst,
scorching wind and sun shall never plague them;
for he who pities them will lead them
and guide them to springs of water.
I will make a highway of all the mountains,
and the high roads shall be banked up.

Some are on their way from afar,
others from the north and the west,
others from the land of Sinim.
Shout for joy, you heavens; exult, you earth!
You mountains, break into happy cries!
For Yahweh consoles his people
and takes pity on those who are afflicted.

Isaiah 60:18-22

Violence will no longer be heard of in your
    country,
nor devastation and ruin within your frontiers.
You will call your walls "Salvation,"
and your gates "Praise."

No more will the sun give you daylight,
nor moonlight shine on you,
but Yahweh will be your everlasting light,
your God will be your splendor.

Your sun will set no more
nor your moon wane,
but Yahweh will be your everlasting light
and your days of mourning will be ended.

Your people will all be upright,
possessing the land for ever;
a shoot that Yahweh has planted,
my handiwork, designed for beauty.

The least among you will become a clan
and the smallest a mighty nation.
I, Yahweh, have spoken;
in due time I shall act with speed.

Isaiah 55:12-13

Yes, you will leave with joy
and be led away in safety.
Mountains and hills will break into joyful cries
*   before you*
and all the trees of the countryside clap their
*   hands.*
Cypress will grow instead of thorns,
myrtle instead of briars.
And this will make Yahweh famous,
a sign for ever, ineffaceable.

Isaiah 42:16

"But I will make the blind walk along the road
and lead them along paths.
I will turn darkness into light before them
and rocky places into level tracks."

Isaiah 25:6-10

On this mountain,
Yahweh Sabaoth will prepare for all peoples
a banquet of rich food, a banquet of fine wines,
of food rich and juicy, of fine strained wines.
On this mountain he will remove
the mourning veil covering all peoples,
and the shroud enwrapping all nations,
he will destroy Death for ever.
The Lord Yahweh will wipe away
the tears from every cheek;
he will take away his people's shame
everywhere on earth,
for Yahweh has said so.
That day, it will be said: See, this is our God
in whom we hoped for salvation;
Yahweh is the one in whom we hoped.
We exult and we rejoice
that he has saved us;
for the hand of Yahweh
rests on this mountain.

Isaiah 12:1-6

> On that day, you will say:
> I give you thanks, O LORD;
>   though you have been angry with me,
>   your anger has abated, and you have consoled me.
> God indeed is my savior;
>   I am confident and unafraid.
> My strength and my courage is the LORD,
>   and he has been my savior.
> With joy you will draw water
>   at the fountain of salvation, and say on that day:
> Give thanks to the LORD, acclaim his name;
>   among the nations make known his deeds,
>   proclaim how exalted is his name.
> Sing praise to the LORD for his glorious
>   achievement;
>   let this be known throughout all the earth.
> Shout with exultation, O city of Zion,
>   for great in your midst
>   is the Holy One of Israel!

(NAB)

Isaiah 7:14

> The Lord himself, therefore,
> will give you a sign.
> It is this: the maiden is with child
> and will soon give birth to a son
> whom she will call Immanuel.

57

Isaiah 26:19

Your dead will come to life,
their corpses will rise;
awake, exult,
all you who lie in the dust,
for your dew is a radiant dew
and the land of ghosts will give birth.

Isaiah 44:3-4

For I will pour out water on the thirsty soil,
streams on the dry ground.
I will pour my spirit on your descendants,
my blessing on your children.
They shall grow like grass where there is
    plenty of water,
like poplars by running streams.

Isaiah 60:1-4

Arise, shine out, for your light has come,
the glory of Yahweh is rising on you,
though night still covers the earth
and darkness the peoples.

Above you Yahweh now rises
and above you his glory appears.
The nations come to your light
and kings to your dawning brightness.

Lift up your eyes and look around:
all are assembling and coming toward you,
your sons from far away
and your daughters being tenderly carried.

Isaiah 41:17-20

The poor and needy ask for water, and there
* is none,*
their tongue is parched with thirst.
I, Yahweh, will answer them,
I, the God of Israel, will not abandon them.

I will make rivers well up on barren heights,
and fountains in the midst of valleys;
turn the wilderness into a lake,
and dry ground into waterspring.

In the wilderness I will put cedar trees,
acacias, myrtles, olives.
In the desert I will plant juniper,
plane tree and cypress side by side;

so that men may see and know,
may all observe and understand
that the hand of Yahweh has done this,
that the Holy One of Israel has created it.

Micah 4:6-7

That day—it is Yahweh who speaks—
I will finally gather in the lame,
and bring together those that have been led astray
and those that have suffered at my hand.
Out of the lame I will make a remnant,
and out of the weary a mighty nation.
Then will Yahweh reign over them
on the mountain of Zion
from now and for ever.

Isaiah 32:15-17

Once more there will be poured on us
the spirit from above;
then shall the wilderness be fertile land
and fertile land become forest.

In the wilderness justice will come to live
and integrity in the fertile land;
integrity will bring peace,
justice give lasting security.

Isaiah 26:1-6

That day, this song will be sung in the land of
    Judah:
We have a strong city;
to guard us he has set
wall and rampart about us.
Open the gates! Let the upright nation come in,
she, the faithful one
whose mind is steadfast, who keeps the peace,
because she trusts in you.
Trust in Yahweh for ever,
for Yahweh is the everlasting Rock;
he has brought low those who lived high up
in the steep citadel;
he brings it down, brings it down to the ground,
flings it down in the dust:
the feet of the lowly, the footsteps of the poor
trample on it.

Isaiah 35:1-10

Let the wilderness and the dry lands exult,
let the wasteland rejoice and bloom,
let it bring forth flowers like the jonquil,
let it rejoice and sing for joy.

The glory of Lebanon is bestowed on it,
the splendor of Carmel and Sharon;
they shall see the glory of Yahweh,
the splendor of our God.

Strengthen all weary hands,
steady all trembling knees
and say to all faint hearts,
"Courage! Do not be afraid.

"Look, your God is coming,
vengeance is coming,
the retribution of God;
he is coming to save you."

Then the eyes of the blind shall be opened,
the ears of the deaf unsealed,
then the lame shall leap like a deer
and the tongues of the dumb sing for joy;

for water gushes in the desert,
streams in the wasteland,
the scorched earth becomes a lake,
the parched land springs of water.

The lairs where the jackals used to live
become thickets of reed and papyrus . . .

And through it will run a highway undefiled
which shall be called the Sacred Way;

the unclean may not travel by it,
nor fools stray along it.

No lion will be there
nor any fierce beast roam about it,
but the redeemed will walk there,
for those Yahweh has ransomed shall return.

They will come to Zion shouting for joy,
everlasting joy on their faces;
joy and gladness will go with them
and sorrow and lament be ended.

Micah 4:1-4

In the days to come
the mountain of the Temple of Yahweh
will be put on top of the mountains
and be lifted higher than the hills.
The peoples will stream to it,
nations without number will come to it;
*   and they will say,*
"Come, let us go up to the mountain of Yahweh,
to the Temple of the God of Jacob
so that he may teach us his ways
and we may walk in his paths;
since from Zion the Law will go out,
and the oracle of Yahweh from Jerusalem."
He will wield authority over many peoples
and arbitrate for mighty nations;
they will hammer their swords into plowshares,
their spears into sickles.
Nation will not lift sword against nation,
there will be no more training for war.
Each man will sit under his vine and his fig tree,
with no one to trouble him.
The mouth of Yahweh Sabaoth has spoken it.

Isaiah 9:1-7

The people that walked in darkness
has seen a great light;
on those who live in a land of deep shadow
a light has shone.
You have made their gladness greater,
you have made their joy increase;
they rejoice in your presence
as men rejoice at harvest time,
as men are happy when they are dividing the
spoils.

For the yoke that was weighing on him,
the bar across his shoulders,
the rod of his oppressor,
these you break as on the day of Midian.

For all the footgear of battle,
every cloak rolled in blood,
is burned,
and consumed by fire.

For there is a child born for us,
a son given to us
and dominion is laid on his shoulders;
and this is the name they give him:
Wonder Counselor, Mighty God,
Eternal Father, Prince of Peace.
Wide is his dominion
in a peace that has no end,
for the throne of David
and for his royal power,
which he establishes and makes secure
in justice and integrity.

From this time onward and for ever,
the jealous love of Yahweh Sabaoth will do this.

Hosea 6:3

"Let us set ourselves to know Yahweh;
that he will come is as certain as the dawn;
his judgment will rise like the light,
he will come to us as showers come,
like spring rains watering the earth."

Isaiah 45:8

Send victory like a dew, you heavens,
and let the clouds rain it down.
Let the earth open
for salvation to spring up.
Let deliverance, too, bud forth
which I, Yahweh, shall create.

Isaiah 27:12-13

That day, Yahweh will start his threshing
from the course of the River to the wadi of Egypt,
and you will be gathered one by one,
sons of Israel.
That day, the great trumpet will be sounded,
and those lost in the land of Assyria will come,
and those exiled to the land of Egypt,
and they will worship Yahweh
on the holy mountain, in Jerusalem.

Isaiah 11:1-9

But a shoot shall sprout from the stump of Jesse,
and from his roots a bud shall blossom.
The spirit of the LORD shall rest upon him:
a spirit of wisdom and of understanding,
A spirit of counsel and of strength.
a spirit of knowledge and of fear of the LORD,
and his delight shall be the fear of the LORD.
Not by appearance shall he judge,
nor by hearsay shall he decide,
But he shall judge the poor with justice,
and decide aright for the land's afflicted.
He shall strike the ruthless with the rod of his
mouth,
and with the breath of his lips he shall slay the
wicked.
Justice shall be the band around his waist,
and faithfulness a belt upon his hips.
Then the wolf shall be a guest of the lamb.
and the leopard shall lie down with the kid;
The calf and the young lion shall browse together,
with a little child to guide them.
The cow and the bear shall be neighbors,
together their young shall rest;
the lion shall eat hay like the ox.
The baby shall play by the cobra's den,
and the child lay his hand on the adder's lair.
There shall be no harm or ruin on all my holy
mountain;
for the earth shall be filled with knowledge
of the LORD,
as water covers the sea.

(NAB)

Joel 4:18

When that day comes,
the mountains will run with new wine
and the hills flow with milk,
and all the river beds of Judah
will run with water.
A fountain will spring from the house of Yahweh
to water the wadi of Acacias.

Zephaniah 3:18-20

I will remove disaster from among you,
* so that none may recount your disgrace.*
Yes, at that time I will deal
* with all who oppress you:*
I will save the lame,
* and assemble the outcasts;*
I will give them praise and renown
* in all the earth, when I bring about their*
*   restoration.*
At that time I will bring you home,
* and at that time I will gather you;*
For I will give you renown and praise,
* among all the peoples of the earth,*
When I bring about your restoration
* before your very eyes, says the LORD.*

(NAB)

Amos 9:13-15

*"The days are coming now—it is Yahweh who
    speaks—*
when harvest will follow directly after plowing,
the treading of grapes soon after sowing,
when the mountains will run with new wine
and the hills all flow with it.
*I mean to restore the fortunes of my people
    Israel;*
*they will rebuild the ruined cities and live in
    them,*
plant vineyards and drink their wine,
dig gardens and eat their produce.
I will plant them in their own country,
never to be rooted up again
out of the land I have given them,
says Yahweh, your God."

Zephaniah 3:14-17

Shout for joy, daughter of Zion,
Israel, shout aloud!
Rejoice, exult with all your heart,
daughter of Jerusalem!
Yahweh has repealed your sentence;
he has driven your enemies away.
Yahweh, the king of Israel, is in your midst;
you have no more evil to fear.

When that day comes, word will come to
*   Jerusalem:*
Zion, have no fear,
do not let your hands fall limp.
Yahweh your God is in your midst,
a victorious warrior.
He will exult with joy over you,
he will renew you by his love;
he will dance with shouts of joy for you
as on a day of festival.

Isaiah 27:2-5

That day,
sing of the delightful vineyard!
I, Yahweh, am its keeper;
every moment I water it
for fear its leaves should fall;
night and day I watch over it.

I am angry no longer.
If thorns and briars come
I will declare war on them,
I will burn them every one.
Or if they would shelter under my protection,
let them make their peace with me,
let them make their peace with me.

Ezekiel 37:1-14

The hand of Yahweh was laid on me, and he carried me away by the spirit of Yahweh and set me down in the middle of a valley, a valley full of bones. He made me walk up and down among them. There were vast quantities of these bones on the ground the whole length of the valley; and they were quite dried up. He said to me, "Son of man, can these bones live?" I said, "You know, Lord Yahweh." He said, "Prophesy over these bones. Say, 'Dry bones, hear the word of Yahweh. The Lord Yahweh says this to these bones: I am now going to make the breath enter you, and you will live. I shall put sinews on you, I shall make flesh grow on you, I shall cover you with skin and give you breath, and you will live; and you will learn that I am Yahweh.' " I prophesied as I had been ordered. While I was prophesying, there was a noise, a sound of clattering; and the bones joined together. I looked, and saw that they were covered with sinews; flesh was growing on them and skin was covering them, but there was no breath in them. He said to me, "Prophesy to the breath; prophesy, son of man. Say to the breath, 'The Lord Yahweh says this: Come from the four winds, breath; breathe on these dead; let them live!' " I prophesied as he had ordered me, and the breath entered them; they came to life again and stood up on their feet, a great, an immense army.

Then he said, "Son of man, these bones are the whole House of Israel. They keep saying, 'Our bones are dried up, our hope has gone; we are as

*good as dead.' So prophesy. Say to them, 'The
Lord Yahweh says this: I am now going to open
your graves; I mean to raise you from your graves,
my people, and lead you back to the soil of Israel.
And you will know that I am Yahweh, when I
open your graves and raise you from your graves,
my people. And I shall put my spirit in you, and
you will live, and I shall resettle you on your own
soil; and you will know that I, Yahweh, have said
and done this—it is the Lord Yahweh who
speaks.' "*

Isaiah 30:18

But Yahweh is waiting to be gracious to you,
to rise and take pity on you,
for Yahweh is a just God;
happy are all who hope in him.

Isaiah 40:28-31

Yahweh is an everlasting God,
he created the boundaries of the earth.
He does not grow tired or weary,
his understanding is beyond fathoming.
He gives strength to the wearied,
he strengthens the powerless.
Young men may grow tired and weary,
youths may stumble,
but those who hope in Yahweh renew their
strength,
they put out wings like eagles.
They run and do not grow weary,
walk and never tire.

Zechariah 9:9-10

Rejoice heartily, O daughter Zion,
* shout for joy, O daughter Jerusalem!*
See, your king shall come to you;
* a just savior is he,*
Meek, and riding on an ass,
* on a colt, the foal of an ass.*
He shall banish the chariot from Ephraim,
* and the horse from Jerusalem;*
The warrior's bow shall be banished,
* and he shall proclaim peace to the nations.*
His dominion shall be from sea to sea,
* and from the River to the ends of the earth.*

(NAB)

Joel 3:1-2

"After this
I will pour out my spirit on all mankind.
Your sons and daughters shall prophesy,
your old men shall dream dreams,
and your young men see visions.
Even on the slaves, men and women,
will I pour out my spirit in those days."

Jeremiah 17:7-8

Blessed is the man who trusts in the LORD,
whose hope is the LORD.
He is like a tree planted beside the waters
that stretches out its roots to the stream:
It fears not the heat when it comes,
its leaves stay green;
In the year of drought it shows no distress,
but still bears fruit.

(NAB)

Implications for Today

The hope expressed in the foregoing selections gives vivid testimony to the profound faith that the prophets had in God's redemptive love and zeal for his people. Despite the desolation that had overtaken the historical moment, the prophets did not waver in the conviction that God was bidding his people both to live anew and to reach out for the realization of what must have seemed an impossible dream.

The people were experiencing the harshest of times, but the scorching wind and sun would never plague them, for God who pitied them would lead and guide them to springs of water. He would wipe away the tears from every cheek and remove their shame everywhere on earth. Yahweh would make rivers well up on barren heights and fountains in the midst of valleys. He would pour out his spirit on all humankind.

The promise of hope, however, also brought a challenge to respond and to take action. If the strength of the people was to be renewed, they must put their trust in God. If there was to be reconciliation, the people must strive to know God and make their peace with him. They must hammer their swords into plowshares and their spears into sickles. If salvation was to be a reality, it must be accepted; faint hearts must put away fear and take up courage.

Such a call to hope is based on belief in God's abiding presence and love even in the darkest moments of one's existence. It is founded on the conviction that the life to which God has called humans transcends all past and present realization. Believers are challenged to let go of present limitations and be open to the life-giving action of the Spirit, who wishes to bring to fulfillment the good work already begun.

For Reflection and Discussion

Identify the most significant symbols that the prophets use in describing the future era of God's abundant blessings.

From the preceding passages, show in what ways the fulfillment of the blessings of the new age depend on the response of the people.

Describe some concrete historical situations in the past 50 years, and in the present day, that are somewhat similar to the plight of the Israelites in the eighth and sixth centuries, B.C. How is the prophetic message of hope applicable in these situations?

Select several specific passages and indicate how the promises expressed in them have been fulfilled. In what way is there room for further fulfillment?

Is hope an unrealistic dream, or is it a virtue that is absolutely necessary for the actualization of our deepest God-given potentials? Explain.

V. God's Mercy

Frequently the prophets had to admonish the Israelites for their sinful conduct and warn of the dire consequences of their unfaithfulness. The reproof, however, was never cause for despair. The God who loved them would never abandon them, even in their sinfulness. God was always calling them back, offering them the opportunity for reconciliation.

Isaiah 1:18

"Come now, let us talk this over,
says Yahweh.
Though your sins are like scarlet,
they shall be as white as snow;
though they are red as crimson,
they shall be like wool."

Joel 2:12-14

"But now, now—it is Yahweh who speaks—
come back to me with all your heart,
fasting, weeping, mourning."
Let your hearts be broken, not your garments
*   torn,*
turn to Yahweh your God again,
for he is all tenderness and compassion,
slow to anger, rich in graciousness,
and ready to relent.
Who knows if he will not turn again, will not
*   relent,*
will not leave a blessing as he passes,
oblation and libation
for Yahweh your God?

Micah 7:18-20

Who is there like you, the God who removes guilt
  and pardons sin for the remnant of his inheri-
    tance;
Who does not persist in anger forever,
  but delights rather in clemency,
And will again have compassion on us,
  treading underfoot our guilt?
You will cast into the depths of the sea
  all our sins;
You will show faithfulness to Jacob,
  and grace to Abraham,
As you have sworn to our fathers
  from days of old.

(NAB)

Isaiah 57:18-19

"But I will heal him, and console him,
I will comfort him to the full,
both him and his afflicted fellows,
bringing praise to their lips.
Peace, peace to far and near,
I will indeed heal him," says Yahweh.

Isaiah 44:21-22

Remember these things, Jacob,
and that you are my servant, Israel.
I have formed you, you are my servant;
Israel, I will not forget you.

I have dispelled your faults like a cloud,
your sins like a mist.
Come back to me, for I have redeemed you.

Micah 7:8-9

Do not gloat over me, my enemy:
though I have fallen, I shall rise;
though I live in darkness,
Yahweh is my light.
I must suffer the anger of Yahweh,
for I have sinned against him,
until he takes up my cause
and rights my wrongs;
he will bring me out into the light
and I shall rejoice to see the rightness of his ways.

Ezekiel 33:11

Answer them: As I live, says the Lord GOD, I swear I take no pleasure in the death of the wicked man, but rather in the wicked man's conversion, that he may live. Turn, turn from your evil ways! Why should you die, O house of Israel?

(NAB)

Isaiah 57:15

"I live in a high and holy place,
but I am also with the contrite and humbled spirit,
to give the humbled spirit new life,
to revive contrite hearts."

Jeremiah 31:31-34

*The days are coming, says the L*ORD, *when I will make a new covenant with the house of Israel and the house of Judah. It will not be like the covenant I made with their fathers the day I took them by the hand to lead them forth from the land of Egypt; for they broke my covenant, and I had to show myself their master, says the L*ORD. *But this is the covenant which I will make with the house of Israel after those days, says the L*ORD. *I will place my law within them, and write it upon their hearts; I will be their God, and they shall be my people. No longer will they have need to teach their friends and kinsmen how to know the L*ORD. *All, from least to greatest, shall know me, says the L*ORD, *for I will forgive their evildoing and remember their sin no more.*

(NAB)

Isaiah 55:6-9

Seek Yahweh while he is still to be found,
call to him while he is still near.
Let the wicked man abandon his way,
the evil man his thoughts.
Let him turn back to Yahweh who will take pity
*   on him,*
to our God who is rich in forgiving;
for my thoughts are not your thoughts,
my ways not your ways—it is Yahweh who
*   speaks.*
Yes, the heavens are as high above earth
as my ways are above your ways,
my thoughts above your thoughts.

Ezekiel 36:25-26

"I shall pour clean water over you and you will be cleansed; I shall cleanse you of all your defilement and all your idols. I shall give you a new heart, and put a new spirit in you; I shall remove the heart of stone from your bodies and give you a heart of flesh instead."

Implications for Today

The prophets believed in a God of tenderness who had power over sin and who was interested not in condemnation, but in comforting sinners and bringing them to new life. The prophetic challenge is not to a preoccupation with one's sinfulness, but rather to a turning back to God with all one's heart.

Popular spirituality by too often emphasizing the destructive consequences of sin has greatly obscured awareness of the healing effects of the redemption. The isolation of a consideration of sin from concentration on God's reconciling love can only lead to a distorted view of the human situation. While it must be acknowledged that humans sin, such a confession can only be adequately made in the context of profound faith that God's forgiveness and love are already at work conquering sin and radically transforming the human heart.

Contemporary psychology has emphasized the role of a good self-image in the development of a balanced personality. From a religious standpoint, one of the most crippling obstacles to a healthy image of self is a guilt complex with its accompanying feeling of worthlessness. Frequent reflection on God's personal acceptance of oneself is more critically necessary for spiritual formation than exhaustive examinations of conscience. The constant struggle in the battle with sin does not necessarily lead to the divine. *Metanoia* must always involve entrusting oneself to a forgiving and compassionate God.

For Reflection and Discussion

Compare the prophetic message in this section with Luke 15:1-32.

From the foregoing passages, select the two that speak to you most strikingly of God's forgiveness and compassion. Explain your choice.

How can the prophetic view of God's mercy aid in coping with guilt feelings?

Often the Sacrament of Reconciliation has come to be identified with confession of sins. In light of this section, how should participation in the Sacrament of Reconciliation be a confession about God?

Describe some of the practical implications that conversion from a "heart of stone" to a "heart of flesh" would have for everyday living.

VI. God's Servant, the Messiah

This section presents the four Songs of the Suffering Servant in Second Isaiah. These songs portray the ideal Servant of God, the perfect Israelite, whose dedication to God's will, even in time of intense suffering, will bring salvation to many. Biblical scholarship has established that the Servant can be interpreted both as the people of Israel and as an individual who is called to play a special role in God's dealings with his people.

Isaiah 42:1-9

Here is my servant whom I uphold,
my chosen one in whom my soul delights.
I have endowed him with my spirit
that he may bring true justice to the nations.

He does not cry out or shout aloud,
or make his voice heard in the streets.
He does not break the crushed reed,
nor quench the wavering flame.

Faithfully he brings true justice;
he will neither waver, nor be crushed
until true justice is established on earth,
for the islands are awaiting his law.

Thus says God, Yahweh,
he who created the heavens and spread them out,
who gave shape to the earth and what comes
*   from it,*
who gave breath to its people
and life to the creatures that move in it:

I, Yahweh, have called you to serve the cause
*   of right;*
I have taken you by the hand and formed you;
I have appointed you as a covenant of the people
*   and light of the nations,*

to open the eyes of the blind,
to free captives from prison,
and those who live in darkness from the dungeon.

My name is Yahweh,
I will not yield my glory to another,
nor my honor to idols.

See how former predictions have come true.
Fresh things I now foretell;
before they appear I tell you of them.

Isaiah 49:1-6

Islands, listen to me,
pay attention, remotest peoples.
Yahweh called me before I was born,
from my mother's womb he pronounced
*   my name.*

He made my mouth a sharp sword,
and hid me in the shadow of his hand.
He made me into a sharpened arrow,
and concealed me in his quiver.

He said to me, "You are my servant (Israel)
in whom I shall be glorified";
while I was thinking, "I have toiled in vain,
I have exhausted myself for nothing";

and all the while my cause was with Yahweh,
my reward with my God.
I was honored in the eyes of Yahweh,
my God was my strength.

And now Yahweh has spoken,
he who formed me in the womb to be his servant,
to bring Jacob back to him,
to gather Israel to him:

"It is not enough for you to be my servant,
to restore the tribes of Jacob and bring back the
*   survivors of Israel;*
I will make you the light of the nations
so that my salvation may reach to the ends of
*   the earth."*

Isaiah 50:4-9

The Lord Yahweh has given me
a disciple's tongue.
So that I may know how to reply to the wearied
he provides me with speech.
Each morning he wakes me to hear,
to listen like a disciple.
The Lord Yahweh has opened my ear.

For my part, I made no resistance
neither did I turn away.
I offered my back to those who struck me,
my cheeks to those who tore at my beard;
I did not cover my face
against insult and spittle.

The Lord Yahweh comes to my help,
so that I am untouched by the insults.
So, too, I set my face like flint;
I know I shall not be shamed.

My vindicator is here at hand. Does anyone
*   start proceedings against me?*
Then let us go to court together.
Who thinks he has a case against me?
Let him approach me.

The Lord Yahweh is coming to my help,
who dare condemn me?
They shall all go to pieces like a garment
devoured by moths.

Isaiah 52:13—53:12

See, my servant will prosper,
he shall be lifted up, exalted, rise to great heights.

As the crowds were appalled on seeing him
—so disfigured did he look
that he seemed no longer human—
so will the crowds be astonished at him,
and kings stand speechless before him;
for they shall see something never told
and witness something never heard before:
"Who could believe what we have heard,
and to whom has the power of Yahweh been
*   revealed?"*
Like a sapling he grew up in front of us,
like a root in arid ground.
Without beauty, without majesty (we saw him),
no looks to attract our eyes;
a thing despised and rejected by men,
a man of sorrows and familiar with suffering,
a man to make people screen their faces;
he was despised and we took no account of him.

And yet ours were the sufferings he bore,
ours the sorrows he carried.
But we, we thought of him as someone punished,
struck by God, and brought low.
Yet he was pierced through for our faults,
crushed for our sins.
On him lies a punishment that brings us peace,
and through his wounds we are healed.

We had all gone astray like sheep,
each taking his own way,
and Yahweh burdened him

with the sins of all of us.
Harshly dealt with, he bore it humbly,
he never opened his mouth,
like a lamb that is led to the slaughterhouse,
like a sheep that is dumb before its shearers
never opening its mouth.

By force and by law he was taken;
would anyone plead his cause?
Yes, he was torn away from the land of the living;
for our faults struck down in death.
They gave him a grave with the wicked,
a tomb with the rich,
though he had done no wrong
and there had been no perjury in his mouth.
Yahweh has been pleased to crush him with
   suffering.
If he offers his life in atonement,
he shall see his heirs, he shall have a long life
and through him what Yahweh wishes will be
   done.

His soul's anguish over
he shall see the light and be content.
By his sufferings shall my servant justify many,
taking their faults on himself.

Hence I will grant whole hordes for his tribute,
he shall divide the spoil with the mighty,
for surrendering himself to death
and letting himself be taken for a sinner,
while he was bearing the faults of many
and praying all the time for sinners.

Implications for Today

The Servant is Israel, alive in all of her eminent leaders and intercessors including Moses, Jeremiah and the suffering exiles. At the same time the songs seem to indicate the coming of an individual Servant of supreme holiness, greater than that of any single Israelite in past history. In the New Testament Jesus Christ is identified as the Servant.

The image of the Servant in these songs challenges many of the accepted norms of human society. According to worldly standards, the powerful and the successful are freed from many of the burdens of service and instead have servants at their disposal. Those in authority are in positions of privilege and can lord it over others. The wealthy and the regal are sheltered from the seamier sides of humanity.

The Servant, on the other hand, serves the cause of human justice. While honored in the eyes of God, he is despised and rejected by the world. Burdened with the sins of humanity, he suffers intensely; and by his suffering he justifies many.

Christ, perceived in light of the Servant Songs, is the only model for Christian discipleship. The essence of the baptismal call is to share in the servant role of Christ. This implies an intimate relationship with God and a compassion for all humanity that is lived out in terms of redemptive involvement in the sufferings of others.

For Reflection and Discussion

What are the main characteristics of the Servant?

What are the most significant aspects of the Servant's mission?

Look up the following New Testament texts: Matthew 8:17; 12:17-21; 26:67; 27:29-31; Mark 1:11; John 1:34; Acts 3:13-26; 8:26-35.

What relevance do the Servant Songs have for understanding the spirituality and the mission of the contemporary Christian?

What kinds of life-style on the part of laity and clergy reflect the Servant image today? What kinds do not?

Who are some of the people in the world today who seem to manifest the Servant image in an extraordinary way? Explain.

Who are the suffering people in your life, and how can you minister to them by compassionate, redemptive involvement in their suffering?

VII. In Praise of God

The Israelite people gradually came to see that the God whose saving power they had experienced, especially in the liberation from Egyptian slavery in the time of Moses, was not merely a tribal god concerned for Israel, but the Lord of the entire universe. Throughout the Hebrew Scriptures there are abundant expressions of praise for God's wonderful works of creation, as well as for his acts of redemption. This theme of honor and glory to Yahweh is also found in the Hebrew prophets.

Isaiah 44:23

Shout for joy, you heavens, for Yahweh has
*   been at work!*
Shout aloud, you earth below!
Shout for joy, you mountains,
and you, forest and all your trees!
For Yahweh has redeemed Jacob
and displayed his glory in Israel.

Amos 5:8

It is he who made the Pleiades and Orion,
who turns the dusk to dawn
and day to darkest night.
He summons the waters of the sea
and pours them over the land.
Yahweh is his name.

Isaiah 40:25-26

"To whom could you liken me
and who could be my equal?" says the Holy One.
Lift your eyes and look.
Who made these stars
if not he who drills them like an army,
calling each one by name?
So mighty is his power, so great his strength,
that not one fails to answer.

Amos 4:13

For he it was who formed the mountains,
    created the wind,
reveals his mind to man,
makes both dawn and dark,
and walks on the top of the heights of the world;
Yahweh, God of Sabaoth, is his name.

Isaiah 25:1-5

Yahweh, you are my God,
I extol you, I praise your name;
for you have carried out your excellent design,
long planned, trustworthy, true.
For you have made the town a heap of stones,
the fortified city a ruin.
The citadel of the proud is a city no longer,
it will never be rebuilt.
Hence a mighty people gives you glory,
the city of pitiless nations holds you in awe;
for you are a refuge for the poor,
a refuge for the needy in distress,
a shelter from the storm,
a shade from the heat;
while the breath of pitiless men
is like the winter storm.
Like drought in a dry land
you will repress the clamor of the proud;
like heat by the shadow of a cloud
the singing of the despots will be subdued.

Isaiah 40:12-14

Who was it measured the water of the sea in
    the hollow of his hand
and calculated the dimensions of the heavens,
gauged the whole earth to the bushel,
weighed the mountains in scales,
the hills in a balance?

Who could have advised the spirit of Yahweh,
what counselor could have instructed him?
Whom has he consulted to enlighten him,
and to learn the path of justice
and discover the most skillful ways?

Isaiah 24:14-16

They lift up their voices, singing for joy;
they acclaim the majesty of Yahweh from the sea.
Therefore in the islands they give glory to Yahweh,
in the islands of the sea, to the name of Yahweh,
    the God of Israel.
From remotest earth we hear songs, "Honor to
    the upright one."

Implications for Today

These prayerful expressions of exultation derive from a contemplative appreciation that all creation and all salvation come from the hands of God. The Lord has power over the sun and the moon and the waters of the sea. He has formed the mountains and created the winds. There is no one who is God's equal either in creative ability or in wisdom.

Moreover, God is a refuge for the poor and for those in distress. He has revealed his mind to humans and has displayed his glory throughout the land. Accordingly, the very heavens and the earth, mountains and forests shout for joy. So, too, should all the people lift up their voices, singing and rejoicing.

The starting point for authentic spirituality is not a preoccupation with religion, perceived as a burden with all its obligations and duties. Genuine growth in relationship with God is founded, rather, on the contemplative experience of God's gift of himself to humans. This gift is manifested in all the magnificence of creation, as well as in God's personal presence in human history.

The appropriate response to such an experience is one of joy and thanksgiving, song and praise. Perhaps too often the wrong virtues have been identified with spirituality, making sanctity seem a glum affair. The foregoing passages underscore the essential place that happiness, gratitude and giving glory to God should have in a life of prayer and holiness.

For Reflection and Discussion

Compare the main themes in these selections with Psalms 135, 146 and 147.

Describe the works of creation attributed to God in this section.

Identify the verses in the foregoing passages that point to the transcendence of God, to how far beyond the reach of human experience he is.

Show how praise, joy and thanksgiving should be an integral part of contemporary prayer and spirituality.

In what concrete ways can the virtue of joy be better manifested in our approach to life, our public worship, our ministering to others?

For my part,
this is my covenant with them,
says Yahweh.
My spirit with which I endowed you,
and my words that I have put in your mouth,
will not disappear from the mouths of your children,
nor from the mouths of your children's children
for ever and ever, says Yahweh.

Isaiah 59:21

Glossary

Acacias: The valley of Shittim, which perhaps may be located near Jerusalem. Shittim means "acacia trees."

Baal: The title applied to several gods, particularly the king of the gods in the Canaanite pantheon. He was a storm-god and a giver of fertility. The Hebrew word *baal* means "lord, master."

Carmel: A mountain near the coast in northwest Palestine.

Ephraim: A territory in the Northern Kingdom, Israel. The name is sometimes used by the prophets as a poetic designation of the Northern Kingdom.

Jacob: Often the prophets use the word *Jacob* as a common designation for Israel.

Lebanon: The chain of mountains which extends north and south along the Syrian coast through the modern country of Lebanon from the Nahr el Kebir until it slopes off in the hills of north Galilee, a distance of about 106 miles. The mountains are named from the Hebrew word which means "white," probably because of the snows which cover the upper slopes of Lebanon most of the year.

Midian: A nomadic tribe. The phrase "on the day of Midian" is an allusion to Israel under Gideon defeating the Midianites during the period of the Judges.

New Moon: A very ancient feast which was, like the Sabbath, a day of rest. It took place on the first day of the new moon. The ritual for the celebration of the New Moon is found in Numbers 28: 11-15.

Orion: A constellation on the equator east of Taurus.

Pleiades: A conspicuous, loose cluster of stars in the constellation Taurus.

Sabaoth: From the Hebrew word which, in Israelite military terminology, means the army drawn from the general population (in contrast to professional soldiers). Yahweh Sabaoth, or Yahweh, God of Sabaoth, means Yahweh, God of armies or God of hosts.

Sharon: The plain of Sharon is the central section of the Palestinian coastal plain, extending roughly from Mt. Carmel in the north to Joppa in the south.

Sinim: Aswan (Assuan), a city in the southern part of Egypt on the east bank of the Nile.

Uzziah: King of Judah, 783-742 B.C.

Yahweh: Name for the God of Israel.

Zion: The southeast hill of Jerusalem which was captured by David and renamed the "City of David." Zion is sometimes used in the Old Testament to signify all of Jerusalem.

Index of Scripture Texts

116